Flying Machines and Their Heroes

AGAINST ALL ODDS
THE GUINEA PIG STORY

BY
Errol Kennedy

First edition 2015
Published by Lundarien Press, UK
Copyright © Errol Kennedy & Imagination Band Ltd 2015

ISBN 978-1-910816-25-7

The right of Errol Kennedy to be identified as the author of this work has been asserted in accordance with the Copyright, Designs and Patents Act 1988

For more info and other books in this series, including this audiobook read by Saul Reichlin, go to:

flyingmachinesandtheirheroes.com

Other Books in the
Flying Machines and Their Heroes Series

1. THE BLENHEIM BOMBER STORY

3. BY DAY AND NIGHT - The B17 and Lancaster Bomber Story

4. TWO LEGENDS OF WWII - The Spitfire and Mustang Story

5. THE PISTON WARRIORS OF WWII

...more to follow soon

Contents

THE GUINEA PIG STORY   7

Appendix 1 - The Advance of Plastic Surgery   52
    through the Ages

Appendix 2 - Profile of Sir Archibald McIndoe   56
    (1900-1960)

THE GUINEA PIG STORY

The spirit of the Guinea Pigs has lived on for sixty years. This is the remarkable story of those heroic men and the vital battles they fought, both in the air and on the ground. Over 600 brave young men, who were never defeated, who rose again to victory and represented the amazing spirit so dear to the nation. In just a few years' time, this very special club will cease to exist. This is truly a story worth telling of how these elite aircrew survived against all odds.

In the late 1930s with Hitler having invaded Europe, it was clear war between Britain and Germany was imminent. Building the preparations for the inevitable war, it became apparent to the RAF that there would undoubtedly be heavy fighting in the sky.

Hundreds and thousands of new aircraft would have to be built, new pilots would have to be trained and unfortunately, as became apparent to the RAF's hierarchy, there were going to be heavy casualties. Fighting in the skies with petrol-laden aircraft would no doubt result in a high rate of badly burnt pilots and aircrew. The treatment of burns and the heavy demand for reconstructive surgery was, at that time, little known territory. It was clearly a time for bold exploration. To help cope with the input of war casualties the Government formed the Emergency Medical Service.

The EMS as it was known, incorporated all of the hospitals throughout England under one emergency service. Huts were built in the grounds of cottage hospitals in rural areas to keep surgery and the treatment of war casualties away from the larger industrial towns, which were under constant threat of enemy bombing.

The reconstructive surgery unit, the EMS, was founded by Sir Harold Gillies, then a prominent plastic surgeon working at St. Bartholomew's Hospital in London. In fact, Sir Harold had been performing plastic surgery since the First World War and is even now considered the founding father of plastic surgery in this country. Gillies chose three surgeons to help him in his operations, bearing in mind that there were only four fully-qualified plastic surgeons working throughout the British Isles at that time. The first he chose was Professor Mowlem, the second, Mr Pomfrey Kilner, and the third his young cousin, who was working alongside him at the time at St. Bartholomew's, Archibald McIndoe.

McIndoe had four years previously tried to gain US citizenship, but he had been turned down. Sir Harold Gillies persuaded him to come back to England and practise and ironically when President Roosevelt heard this, he revoked the original decision and offered him citizenship and McIndoe turned it down.

Each of the three surgeons was given one of the cottage hospitals to set up a unit in preparation for the flow of casualties. Archibald McIndoe chose the Queen Victoria Cottage Hospital at East Grinstead. In 1938, three wooden huts and a kitchen were built in the hospital grounds, wards 1, 2 and 3, awaiting a surgeon to take them on.

When Archibald McIndoe came along, what transpired over the following years was the creation of a legend and what can only be regarded as one of the curiosities of the war.

Cyril Jones: "It was just a very ordinary, modern cottage hospital run by the local people, so therefore I knew nothing at all and went there keen and interested, but not expecting what happened. McIndoe was the honorary plastic surgeon to the Air Force and he used to visit the Air Force hospitals throughout England. He used to leave on a Monday morning from Gatwick, a little flying area, which is now the gigantic airport, and he used to go round to all the existing RAF hospitals. Whilst visiting these hospitals he sometimes left instructions, after meeting badly burnt aircrew,

that they should be transferred to East Grinstead. He was the leading light who had a very good team of people behind him."

Percy Jayes Surgent: "When the war started, McIndoe asked me if I would come to East Grinstead and I came down to the hospital in March 1940."

Sister Meely: "We were a happy band of nurses you know, we were lucky because McIndoe made sure

there were plenty of nurses there. There were ten of us, I think, and we all worked together. I always felt it was one of my happiest times in my life".

The first trickle of patients to the Queen Victoria Hospital were young dispatch riders and pilots injured during training accidents - there were even odd casualties from the phoney war. But by the summer of 1940, Archy McIndoe and his team realised they were going to be under severe pressure. The trickle turned into a flood and the now-famous Ward 3 was to become the home to many unfortunate young airmen, for in the skies over this country all out war was raging; it was the Battle of Britain.

Churchill's few fought a relentless battle. The

average RAF pilot in the summer of 1940 was a little over 20 years of age. He was unmarried and had not quite finished his formal education. He had a passion for fast cars, pretty women and aeroplanes. He had joined the RAF less than ten months before becoming operational and would have had less than twenty hours experience on the Hurricane and Spitfire types.

Because of the large amounts of fuel carried, badly burnt pilots became more commonplace and because of the position of the fuel tanks, Hurricane pilots were most at risk. In fact, staff at East Grinstead became very familiar with the standard Hurricane burn.

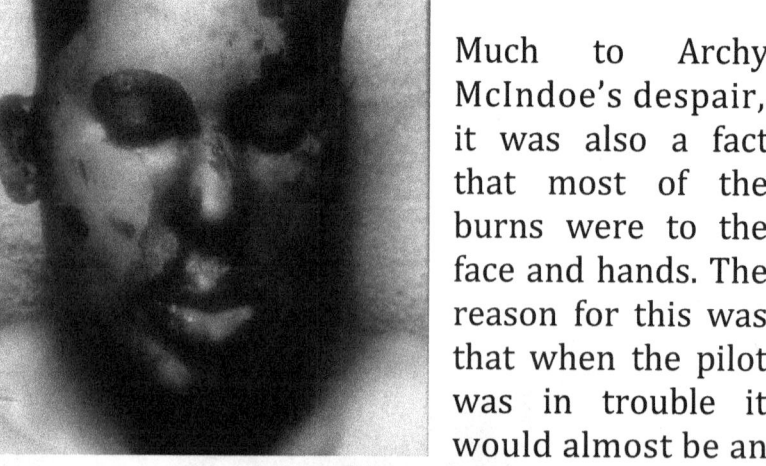

Much to Archy McIndoe's despair, it was also a fact that most of the burns were to the face and hands. The reason for this was that when the pilot was in trouble it would almost be an automatic reaction to remove his goggles and gloves, thus removing what protection he had from the flames. One of the first pilots from the Battle of Britain to reach East Grinstead and Ward 3 was Thomas Gleave.

Group Captain Thomas Gleave C.B.E.: "We arrived on the 29th August in time for the bloodiest forty eight hours of the battle which was the 30th and 31st August. In that short period, we suffered heavy losses through heavy fighting and, on the 31st, the Commanding Officer of the Squadron was killed. I handed over to him a fortnight before and was allowed to stay with the Squadron. I was set on fire at midday and so another CO came in, totalling three in one day.

"It is very hard to say how you were hit, I heard a 'ping' and my starboard tank caught fire and the problem with the wing tank catching fire is that inevitably the suction would draw the flames into the fuselage. I was sitting on the right hand wing, which meant the flames hit the left hand side of the cockpit, coming over your right shoulder and of course vice versa. That is why my right leg was completely burnt, more so than my left leg. The side of my face was also burnt as well as my nose and eyelids, which did not disappear but just shrivelled away. If I had been in a Spitfire which had the main tank in front of you, that being 60 gallons, and 35 gallons I think on top; if I had not have got out in the first five seconds I would have had it, so the Hurricane had this advantage, you had a chance to get out. I never got out as I was struggling with my hood, then it blew up and I was blown out. So it was the lazy man's way of getting out! Luckily my parachute worked."

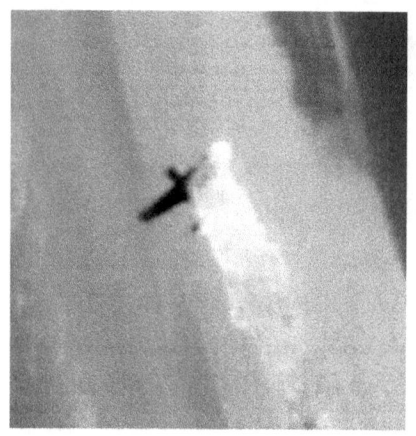

Tom managed to pull his ripcord and came down over a farm just outside Biggin Hill; he was taken to Orpington where they saved his life. His face, hands, arms and legs were treated in tannic acid, one of the only known treatments at the time for severe burns. He had only been at Orpington for a couple of weeks when he heard of a special burns unit at East Grinstead. There was also a surgeon there that specialised in plastic surgery and skin grafts, Archibald McIndoe. McIndoe discovered early on that the burns of pilots who came down over the sea healed a lot quicker than those that came down over the land. So he developed the salt bath treatment for his patients and Tom Gleave was transferred to East Grinstead.

Tom Gleave: "I felt I was getting better because I was driven down by a very pretty ATS girl and the very fact that I noticed what she looked like, showed I was on the mend; we got on very well. She took me down to East Grinstead, I had a cage over my legs and all these bandages on, some had been on for days, because, what happened was, a bit like linen, the little granules of flesh pushed up through the squares in the bandages and spread so it would not come off, it was absolute hell.

I got down there and Sister Meely from Ward 3 who is here having drinks with us, bless her, arranged that I went in the bath at 4.00 pm and outwardly I was a picture of fantastic courage, but inside I was scared stiff. I did not know what was going to happen, I got into the salt water and it was unbelievable, the pain went and the bandages floated off and you could almost feel the skin starting to heal. Then what they did, in fact Percy who did my legs for me, who is also here, put rows and rows of grafts down my legs, I still have the places that they came from and each time I went into the salt bath you could see the little milky skin growing between the grafts and my legs were covered in about ten days, mind you it was very, very thin skin but it was covered. It was marvellous, Sister Marron, a dear lady, a naval Matron in World War I, a lovely lady, awoke me whilst my legs were in the cage and pulled the sheets off and watered my legs with a watering can of warm saline. I thought I had either been to a guest night or out with the boys and had bottle of gin from under my pillow or something, but it dawned on me it was dear old Marron doing this for me. I said, 'What are you doing this for?' and she replied, 'The bandages must be kept damp at all costs.' so I had this done every night for quite a long time."

As with a great many of the patients at East Grinstead, Tom Gleave's face was a mess, he had lost his eyelids and his nose had been completely burnt away. Some of the others had lost all recognisable features.

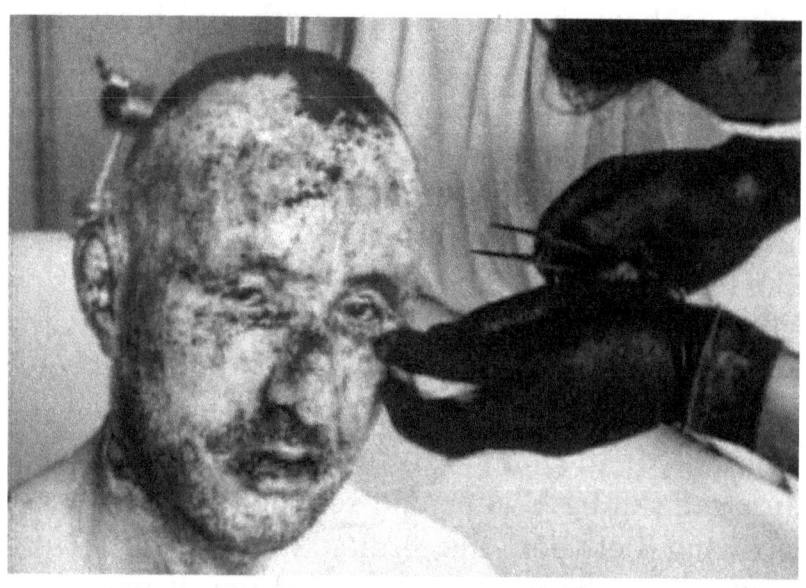

Those frightened young men, entering Ward 3 for

the first time, found it hard to accept that they were going to be horrendously disfigured for the rest of their lives.

When Archy McIndoe examined Tom Gleave's face, he said we can do either one of two things: we can give your nose a skin graft to give it some sort of covering or we can give it a new nose. It will be a long job but it will be worth it. Tom Gleave chose a new nose.

Cyril Jones: "It was mainly hands and faces that we saw, so therefore surgery was mainly to return the functions of the face, not to make anyone look pretty again, but for its original uses, in other words so that they can open and close their eyes and mouth and give them some kind of ear in order for them to put their glasses on."

McIndoe realised very early on that not only did he have the job of making whole the mutilated bits and pieces of these young airmen, but he had to get them back into society and for them to accept the way they were. Now, to do that, he had to have their confidence not only in him as a surgeon, but they also had to have confidence in themselves. He encouraged a common bond of comradeship within the hospital.

East Grinstead was not to have all the pomp and regulations that existed in other Military hospitals and what happened was a kind of hospital life that shook the medical profession and hierarchy. Rank, rules and regulations were all forgotten, everyone was equal, even the staff in McIndoe's hospital and nothing was going to stand in the way of making his boys, as he called them, whole again.

Cyril Jones: "McIndoe never did anything that he had not thought out properly, he was a very far-seeing man who had seen these boys in his mind in fifty years time and he knew damn well that he could not return them to look like film stars but he did know that they must get back into public life if they were going to make any good at all."

McIndoe allowed his boys the freedom they deserved. Beer was allowed in the ward, they could visit the local pubs in the evening usually in wheelchairs pushed by the nurses. They could wake up when they wished, he even did away with the regulation hospital blues and allowed them to wear their own uniforms. The men loved him. They could talk with him whenever they wished, again something which was previously unheard of in a military hospital. He became known as "the Boss".

So it came about one evening in June 1941 when several patients were sat around discussing their grafts during a drinking session in Ward 3, they decided that they were a group of rather exclusive individuals. The idea of a club was banded around and what better name to call it than the Guinea Pig Club?

Tom Gleave was in at that meeting, he became one of the founder members of the club. In fact he is now Chief Guinea Pig. McIndoe thought the idea of the club was an excellent way to encourage the camaraderie between his men and gave them all the support that they wanted.

What started out as almost a joke and perhaps just an excuse for another weekly drinking session, in fact gave these young men a new purpose to their lives. Another of the founder members was Wing Commander Derek Martin.

Derek Martin: "In March 1941, I was returning from a flight out in the mid-Atlantic, looking for submarines at night. I ran into bad weather and crashed into the North Atlantic off Hoburn on the west coast of Scotland, and we went down and about half the crew were killed in the crash. I was eventually fished out of the water and I remember lying on the deck of the boat that fished me out and hearing Italian voices say, "This one's dead," and having a blanket thrown over me. When I arrived at East Grinstead I went first into the main hospital, the Kindersley Ward. I was too ill to go into Ward 3 and I was there for quite a long time before I could be moved into Ward 3 for the actual plastic surgery. From then on McIndoe was putting my scalp and my face back together again."

Derek Martin wasn't burnt, but he almost lost the top of his scalp and his left eye was out of its socket.

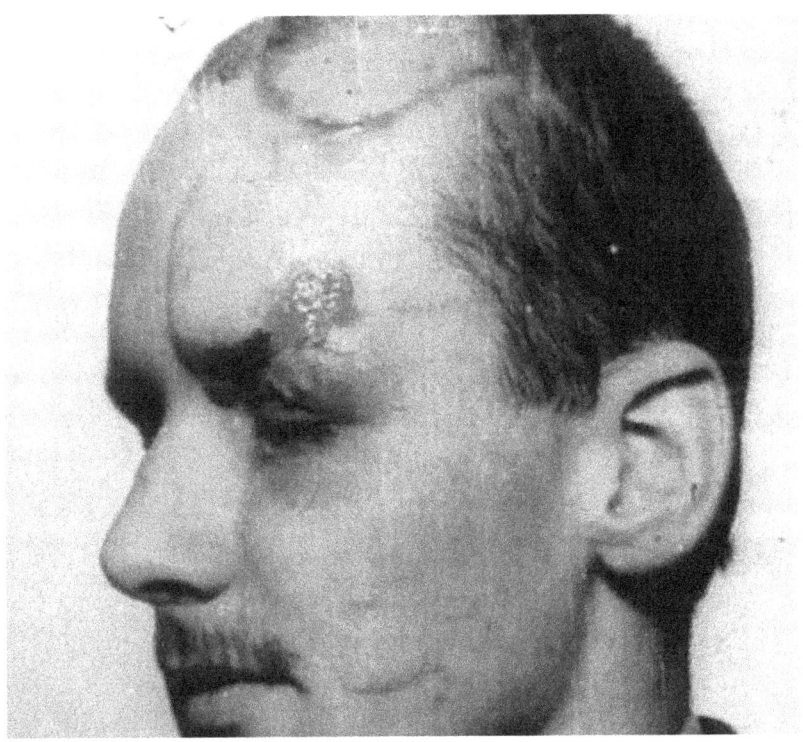

To be admitted to East Grinstead you had to be fried, mashed or boiled. Derek Martin had been mashed. He arrived at the Queen Victoria Hospital in April 1941, where he was immediately treated by McIndoe with an ingenious new development of the salt bath treatment, which was the saline irrigation system. McIndoe's skill as a surgeon was brilliant. As well as being known as the 'Boss', he also earned the title the 'Maestro'.

Bomber Command's losses were high, the casualties coming into the Queen Victoria at East Grinstead were now a different breed of men; not only were they the young fighter pilots but also the aircrew of bomber and coastal commands, and this was to continue for the rest of the war.

Archy McIndoe and his team fought their own relentless battle throughout the war, no less than 649 men became Guinea Pigs and not one of them was treated any different to the other, and the men found that upon entering the Queen Victoria Hospital they noticed the unique approach in caring for the patients. Archy McIndoe's team immediately took the men to their hearts.

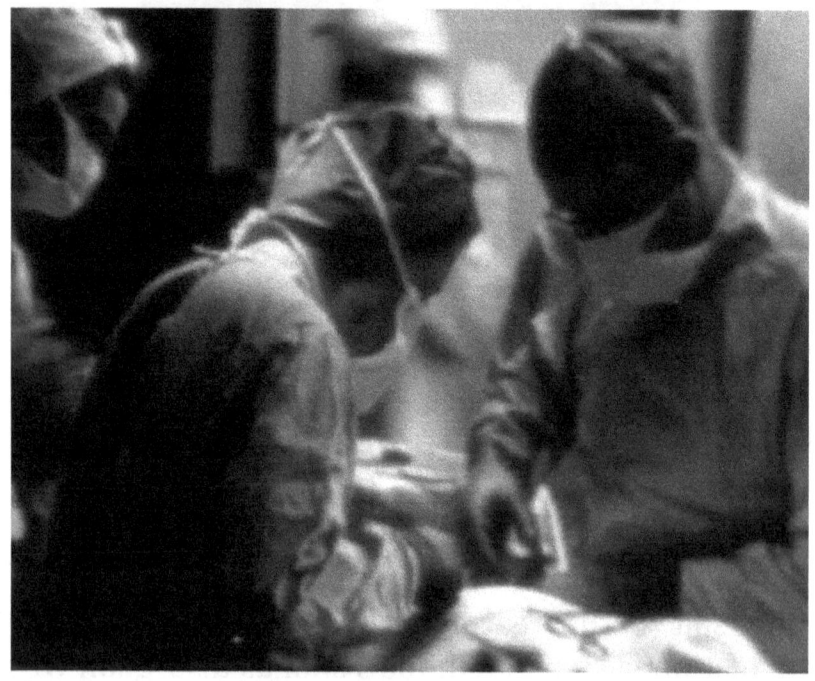

John Hunter, a brilliant anaesthetist who joined Archy from the very beginning, Dr Russell Davis a Consultant Anaesthetist to the hospital, a medical liaison officer to the Guinea Pig Club and a champion for their cause in later years.

One of the team, who is sadly no longer alive, was Edward Blaxell (Blacky).

Blacky was posted to East Grinstead as a PT instructor with the RAF. On arrival to the unit he was laying out his PT shoes and shirt on the bed in Ward 3, when a legless and horrified Guinea Pig exclaimed, "Good god, you are not, well, doing PT with us?" He never did. He soon realised that he enjoyed a pint of beer as much as they did. He was an instant success amongst the men helping them come to terms with their injuries and looking after their welfare.

Matron Hall had a tough job. The problem was that although these men were badly mutilated, mentally they were fit and by being cooped up in hospital for such a long period of time they developed an almost black sense of humour. The matron, whom they all loved, was quite often on the receiving end of their antics.

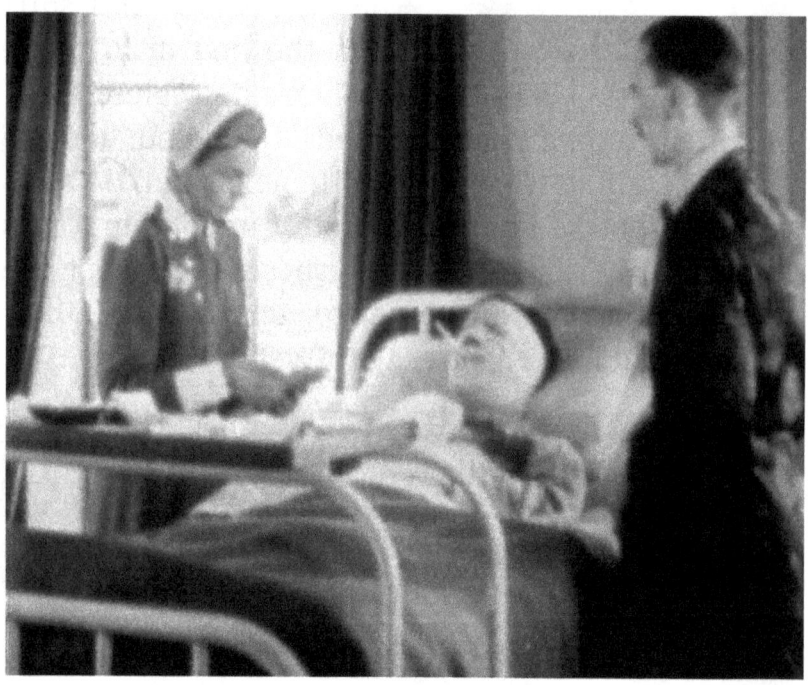

Cyril Jones: "The Matron we had was the matron that I first started with, when the hospital first opened, in 1937 and she was a dear thing. She was an Irish lady who was very dedicated and she thought the world of us all. Thought the world of me. In fact she was like my Mum for a long time. She was suddenly confronted by these young, fit men, who were badly burnt, who did things which she did not think was correct. She woke up one morning and looked out of the window down into the forecourt of the hospital, which had a round bed in it, and she saw half a dozen Belisha beacons that had been taken out from the town and put round her bed. She wondered what had hit her! From then on she accepted everything. In fact she came down several months later and in the main hall was a big piece of furniture which had been brought up with all the patron's hats, coats, umbrellas, walking sticks and boots on it and placed in the hall of the hospital. No one knew how it got there until they actually went along the corridor and found a buffalo horn with a six foot wing span on it. I suppose it was just high spirits. The local police were very understanding and helpful. They would not get away with it nowadays."

Sister Meely: "Very nice woman, very gentle and in fact she used to get embarrassed on our ward. They were very respectful to her as a matron of course."

Another recruit at the exclusive Guinea Pig Club was Jimmy Wright.

Blinded by his wartime injuries as well as being badly burnt, he now leads a career as a film producer. Jimmy Wright was a wartime photographer for the Royal

Air Force. When the photo-reconnaissance Marauder that he was flying in crashed over Italy, a strange course of events took place.

Jimmy was taken to an army hospital delirious from pain, and all he could remember was hearing the voices of Italians and being in constant agony. In fact the Italians were prisoners of war being used as stretcher bearers, but in Jimmy's mind he was being tortured in a prisoner of war camp. Back in England Jimmy's mother had received a telegram saying that her son had been killed in action. Jimmy's father, a war correspondent, found out differently. He was immediately taken to East Grinstead.

Jimmy Wright: "I had a tremendous amount of pain in the right eye because. having lost the eyelids, the eye was exposed and had been rather badly burnt. I always remember that he had done a day's surgery and he was doing the ward round. He took one look at my right eye and said he would see me later on in the evening. He came back with his anaesthetist and John Mullins, his theatre assistant, and put some skin over the right eye to relieve the pain. That was the kind of person he was, he didn't spare himself at all, he was absolutely tremendous."

Whenever Archy McIndoe wanted to show off his handiwork, one of the Guinea Pigs was always sent for. Jack was a wireless operator in a Hamden Bomber, when his aircraft was shot down while attempting to land in Norfolk. He was the sole survivor.

Jack Allaway: "Well, I remember us coming down, having been shot down, returning from a bombing mission. As we crashed into the field, the aircraft just burst into flames and there was the scramble to try and get out of the aircraft and I realised that I was not going to make it. All those fleeting thoughts came into my head of my mother and father and the feelings they would have of not seeing me return home. I had no fear of dying at all, just lots of thoughts flashing through my mind, and suddenly I saw daylight, and we had come down over a ditch, so instead of trying to get out at the top of the aircraft I dropped out of the bottom which had been completely ripped apart. I started running across the field looking at my hands and seeing all the skin hanging from the fingers and turning round just looking at the aircraft."

The Maestro's work on Jack involved over forty operations.

Percy Jayes Surgent: "As long as there are big open wounds, the patients are losing fluid and their general condition is difficult to maintain. Once the surfaces are covered with skin their general health begins to improve, their weight increases and they are well on the way to recovery."

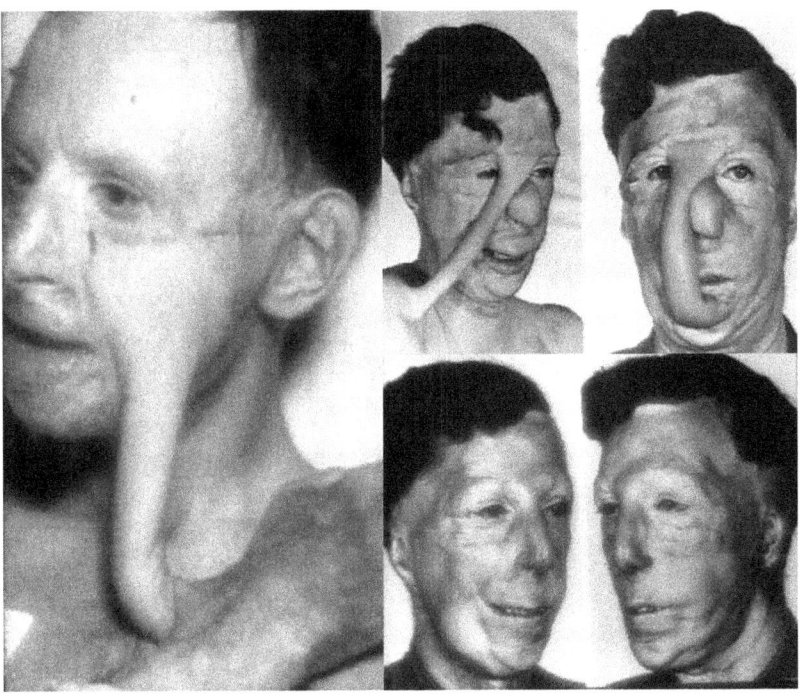

Then they started the actual reconstruction of eyelids, nose or whatever it might be. This might entail perhaps a whole face being reconstructed over many separate operations. In other cases where there had been deep destruction, a loss not only of skin but also of fatty tissue and substance. It was then necessary to transfer a whole pedicle of skin in order to build up the normal contours. This was done with pedicle flaps so you sometimes found a patient had to go around for a while with a tube of skin, taken from his chest, running from over his shoulder onto his nose."

His dictum of encouraging the patient and giving him a sense of confidence helped Jack through the four-year period in hospital.

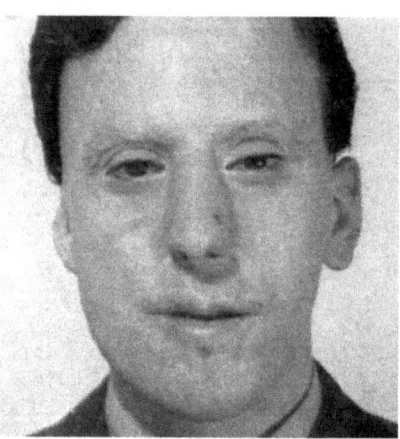

Jack Allaway: "You are feeling pretty low at the time and you are aware that there are going to be several years of plastic surgery treatment to come. Sir Archy McIndoe came along with this patient and he was a pilot who had been burnt in 1936. He stood him by the side of my bed and said, "Jack, by the time I have finished with you this is what you will look like." He inspired us all. I do not think I ever looked back after that."

As the war continued so did the casualties amongst airmen and aircrew. Because of the extent of time needed to treat each patient, in some cases involving many years of surgery, Ward 3 was being used to its utmost capacity.

The Guinea Pig Club was one of Britain's best success stories. Who could have decreed that at the outset of war that we should put all the burnt airmen in an uncomfortable wooden hut where they would create an amazing spirit and bring it back to the nation? To help the chaps we shall recruit the prettiest nurses, find a matron who welcomes beer on the wards and will allow her patients out in the evenings to visit the night clubs. We shall put a New Zealander named McIndoe in charge who seems not only capable of carving people up but is also able to understand their minds. Here these men will form a club and a bond that will last for the rest of their lives.

Jim Sandiman Allen D.FM.: "As the Guinea Pig Club is formed from a group of airmen of English, Canadian or Australians, any of the allied forces who were injured during the 1939-45 war, and during that period came to the Queen Victoria Hospital in East Grinstead where they had surgery by Sir Archibald McIndoe or one of his assistants."

Jim Sandiman Allen was a mashed Guinea Pig. In his career before ending up at East Grinstead, he crashed his Hurricane fighters twice, had been wounded in combat over Singapore and had finally been shot up rather badly when a shell entered the cockpit of his Typhoon over France. Despite horrific injuries - his leg was shattered, his arm was almost severed - he managed to fly the Typhoon back to England and land safely.

Jim: "Well I have rather a large hole in my leg, I am full of metal and this arm was shattered and I flew back with it swinging and all the ends of the bone grinding, which was more than a bit uncomfortable, but it kept me awake. I knew I'd got to land and finish and I landed more by good luck than judgement. I just sat there and thought, 'Thank God, I am home.'"

But that wasn't the end of Jim's combat career before ending up at East Grinstead.

Jim: "Eventually they allowed me back on the squadron on crutches and I was allowed to fly again, which was very decent of them. This lasted for a few weeks until my wounds went wrong on me, not to my knowledge though. I was transferred away for a break. On my way, I was sent to the fighter headquarters, which was Bentley Priory, which was full of all the big wigs and scrambled egg. I got there one day, I had my own little motorcar, and felt terrible and I decided I would go sick and I drove down to where the sick bay was, parked my car and went in. I was sitting around and one of the doctors came round, took a look and disappeared. Then a little while later a stretcher party came in and went rushing in to the doctor, but they picked me up. Ten days later I returned and found that I had parked my car in the local commanding officer's car park and I was in terrible trouble. Anyway, I got through all that of course, went back again to flying. That did not last long, things went wrong again and I was sent to East Grinstead, where Archy sorted me out, and then I was invalided out of the Air Force."

Another of Archie's Guinea Pigs was Jack Toper.

Jack was returning from a mission in a Wellington Bomber when it crash-landed at Clacton-on-Sea.

Jack Toper: "Jill Mullins was the sister in the operating theatre and worked with Sir Archibald McIndoe. In her role as operating theatre sister - she was also quite a wonderful person in so many other ways - when we went into the theatre to have our operations she would make sure that hearts would stop fluttering. I always remember very well this beautiful red headed lady who used to stroke our hair and it really was quite a privilege to go under with her standing there. She was marvellous and it was a great pity that she died such a young lady because, like Sir Archibald McIndoe, she had a great deal to offer."

With war raging in all corners of the globe, brave men from all dominions of the empire crossed thousands of miles to defend their mother country.

Fire does not differentiate, their bodies burned just as easily. They came in such numbers that very soon they were in as much need of Ward 3 as the British. The Guinea Pigs not only came from the Royal Air Force but also from Czechoslovakia,

Poland, New Zealand, Australia and, perhaps most of all remembered, the Canadians. As the Canadian casualties poured in, it grew plain to see that this bursting cottage hospital could not continue to operate its special facilities. The Canadian Government responded swiftly to the problem. They sent in the Canadian engineers with all the materials. In a very short space of time East Grinstead had a large brick built new wing. They even sent the personnel to staff it. Even today the hospital has retained its unique friendly atmosphere. The dictum of Sir Archibald McIndoe has remained still as strong today as it ever was.

Hank Hastings: "I was taken in a wheelchair down to eat with the rest of the fellows and noticed the rest of them down there and how happy they were despite very serious injuries and burns. It seemed the more injured they were, the happier they were. So if you did feel sorry for yourself up to that point, you certainly did not have to. Of course the nurses were always exceptionally good to us. They used to take us down to the White Hall at night to the pub and wheel us back again."

A local lady who worked as a volunteer for the hospital during the war years still works there today. Ann Standen has been a working friend of the Guinea Pigs for nearly fifty years; she remembers them all fondly. None more than her deceased husband, Guinea Pig Henry Standen.

Ann Standen: "Of course at that time you know there were severe blackouts. They were all ready  to leave the field and one of our own planes came in to land and just tipped their plane. Of course the whole lot went up on the field. Henry apparently had the presence of mind to throw himself further down the bank.

Everybody was killed instantly, except Henry. He was as right as rain for three whole days before the shock set in. Then they took him the Rawsbury. Archy then saw him, as he used to visit there, and he was sent down to East Grinstead like most of the boys. At the time of his death I think he had had seventy-one operations altogether."

Ann wasn't the only member of staff at East Grinstead to marry a Guinea Pig, Sister Meely dearly loved and remembered for the gentle way she treated her patients married Bucky. They have been happily married ever since.

Bucky: "I remember being a bit pessimistic. I thought it would not last, but it did not of course, it just went from strength to strength."

Jack Toper: "Sister Meely was quite a character. Anyone who went into Ward 3 would have to meet Sister Meely. She ruled the ward, but not in the true sense of governing, she was charm itself. Her Irish brogue used to thrill us when we went in there and, I was telling her last night actually, she had the reputation of having the most gentlest hands of all the nursing people I had come across. By that, I mean, when we had our ops she used to remove the stitches and I have never known anyone to remove stitches so gently as that lady. Fortunately we have seen her this year, she came down to join us for the reunion and it's just like old times: hugs and kisses, lots of chatter and quite a lovely lady. "

Alan Morgant: "We took off for Stuttgart on my 21st Birthday in the evening, as we were going to bomb Stuttgart. Over the target we got heavy flack that blew the door open. The pilot asked the wireless operator to see if he could close the door. He had nothing to do at that particular time.

He went down with his emergency oxygen bottle, got to the door, blacked out because the oxygen bottle, instead of lasting twelve minutes, was only half full. The skipper said, 'Alan, go and see what has happened to Frank.' So I grabbed the emergency bottle, clipped on my mask and went down, found Frank unconscious, took my gloves off to fix him up with the oxygen and managed to drag him over the fuselage, over the raised bar, and plugged him into his own supply of oxygen. He recovered and, when he was okay, I went down to close the door. When I got to the door unfortunately my bottle packed up too, so I collapsed unconscious for about three to five minutes. In that short time it was below -43° at 23,000 feet and I got severe frostbite in my hands.

"So McIndoe must have been on his rounds and they brought me to Queen Victoria Hospital in East Grinstead. They immediately put both arms in two big ice buckets over my bed. The reason for that was to gradually thaw them out, but when they took them out of the ice bucket after about six days, there was no chance.

"So the next day, Ross Tilley, the Canadian surgeon, took charge. He was in charge of the ice buckets and I believe he was instrumental in designing and cutting my fingers back into the palms of my hands and using my knuckles as stumps for fingers.

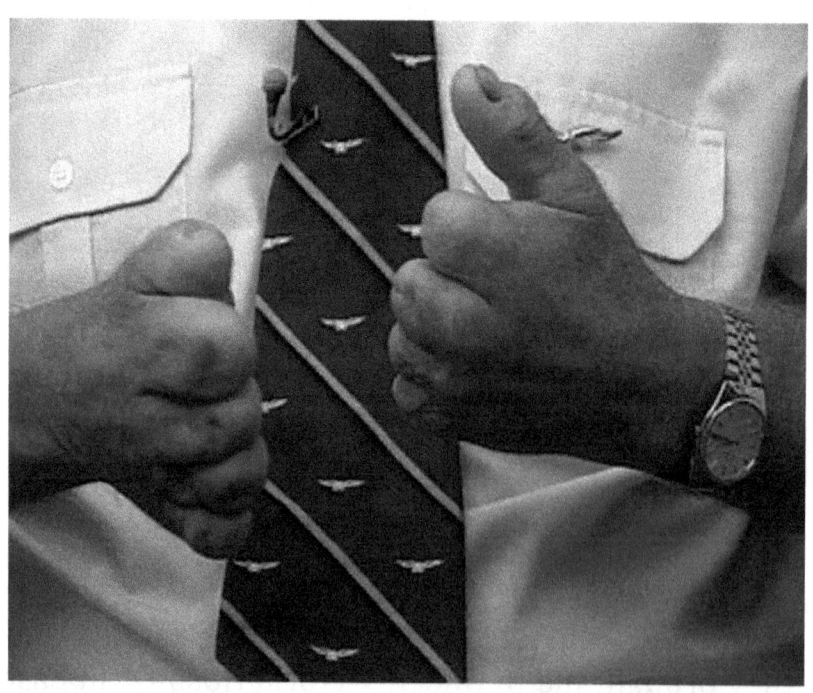

"When I came out, I immediately went back to my

old firm as a skilled toolmaker and I have worked for forty-odd years with my hands.

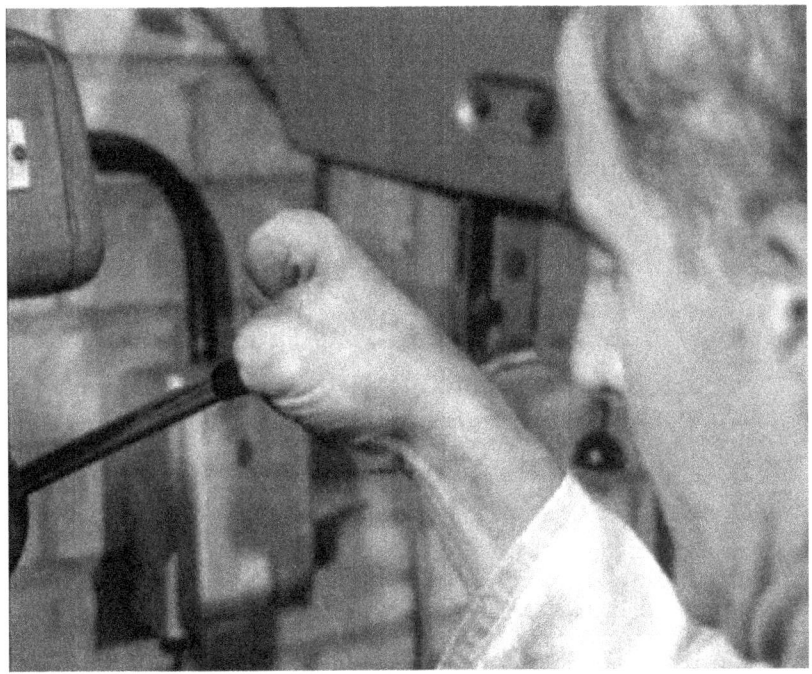

"I have two sons, one is a skilled chartered engineer and the other son is a dental surgeon. From them, I have five grand children and a wonderful wife. We are now just having a smashing time, going on holidays with the caravan and booking holidays abroad whenever we can. Were just having a wonderful time. At first, I was very ill, but after about six weeks my impressions were that we used to gang together particularly three of us; there was Les Wilkins, Bill Foxley, myself who would pal together. It was a matter of going down to the White Hall, never paying for a drink, getting really canned and coming back to the hospital. Sister Meely would provide us with bread, toast and fried bread particularly. It was like a holiday, it was home from home. Sister Meely is here now at this 50th Anniversary and, until this year, we've never seen her for 47 years. I must say that through Sister Meely nursing me through six weeks of pneumonia when I first arrived in Ward 3, I owe my life to Sister Meely and I will never forget her."

Archy McIndoe encouraged wherever he could for the boys to meet girls, allowing them to go out into East Grinstead and even up to London, usually accompanied by Blacky or Cyril Jones. Needless to say, they did not need much encouragement.

Cyril Jones: "The boys seemed to attract very attractive women despite their badly burnt bodies - more so than ordinary civilians who were not burnt. Also a lot of them were very happily married for the rest of their lives. So I do not believe that scars on men's faces, providing they have a personality, have adverse effects and they do just as well as ordinary men in the street. They went through a psychological era just after they were burnt and a lot of them almost became suicidal. I think the reason why they were nursed out of this was because they were always all together at East Grinstead and could always find someone who was worse off than they were. There were a terrific number of invitations to these boys but McIndoe insisted on a member of the RAF Medical Team going with them.

"I can remember at the time that Mai West was in a

show in town and, of course, once it was realised that these types of boys were there, we were always invited round the back to meet all the stars and have drinks with them. Mai West was fantastic. She thought the boys were wonderful and vice versa. Once the boys had too much to drink, the debutantes or the ladies of the set used to disappear and I was left with a few boys and had to get them back to East Grinstead and that could be difficult. Anyone who was anyone who visited England came to East Grinstead. Many of the very well-known actors and actresses came to see the boys. McIndoe was insistent that his theatre staff met every one of them. They were taken around this fantastic theatre and even down to the boiler room. He was so proud of his achievements. We had men like Clark Gable visiting, who was then a Colonel in the Air Force in the USA. Also I remember Gregory Peck, Merle Oberon and Mai West. I was lucky, I was presented to the Queen Mother twice and we had the foreign royalty over and I seem to remember three kings and a few princes and princesses, we had to meet them all, it was our duty." They were so proud.

Since the war the Guinea Pig Club has gone from strength to strength. Every year the members meet for their annual reunion weekend, starting with a party on Friday evening and ending with lunchtime drinks on Sunday. The Guinea Pigs reminisce and exchange experience of their wartime enemies and peacetime disabilities.

They discuss their years of struggle for reasonable pensions. Archy McIndoe's dictum of the Guinea Pigs standing by each other has reined with them for fifty years. They are always constantly aware that the horrific injuries they received have become, for some of the Guinea Pigs, increasingly difficult to bear as they get older.

George Ullison for example, now suffering from a recent stroke, is being cared for by the Royal Air Force's Association at their home in Sussex. George is a Guinea Pig and will remain under his fellow Guinea Pigs' watchful eye for the rest of his life.

For not only do 'guinea pigs' help each other but they have also been invaluable to other burns victims. Simon Weston, burnt during the Falklands conflict, was one of them.

Jack Toper: "We try and do what we can. We help each other of course as a club, but what we like to do, although in many respects we are restricted, is we like to help other unfortunate people who have been burnt, disfigured. When you think of it we have had to live with our disfigurement for over 50 years and who but us could give a complete knowledge to other patients? Now, when there are disasters, for example like the Falklands War, we got in touch with the Chief of Defence staff and they agreed that some Guinea Pigs should go along and see if we could help these chaps as they came back from the Falklands. One chap in particular, Simon Weston, whom everyone must know about by now, was very badly burnt and I suppose really I took him under my wing and went up to visit him at the Queen Elizabeth Military Hospital at Woolwich. I like to think that, by visiting him a few times, telling him what it was like, how he would have to cope with fingers that had been mashed about a bit, convoluted, I would like to think that what I said to him was of value to him. I think it was and that we as a club did help him."

Sadly in 1960, Archy McIndoe, having been knighted for his services, died at an early age, leaving behind him his wife and a legend. Up until the time of his death he had been the President of the Guinea Pig Club, a role that is now carried on by his Royal Highness Prince Phillip, who has continued in this capacity to this very day.

The Boss was going to be sadly missed, not only by his Guinea Pigs, but also by all those who had the pleasure to come into contact with him. He had always wanted the best for his men and had fought relentlessly to ensure nothing or nobody stood in the way of making them whole again. He knew that social disability was going to be their greatest handicap and he installed in each and every one of them that will power to want to do more than just succeed. Perhaps it could be said that he <u>made</u> the Guinea Pigs. He would have preferred to think the Guinea Pigs made him.

What started out as an excuse for a few badly injured airmen to get together for a drink, very soon bonded together over 600 men from all walks of life into a fellowship that would decree, up until the day that the last Guinea Pig died, another Guinea Pig would never be in need.

Jack Allaway: "He was a wonderful man, a wonderful surgeon, a wonderful philosopher. He meant everything to us, all the patients, he was God. We looked to him as our saviour and the best years of our lives were possibly spent at the Queen Victoria Hospital with Archy McIndoe."

Jack Toper: "I think, quite simply, it's very simple: through adversity comes strength. Now if you are having a tough time on your own it is difficult, but do not forget that the number of Guinea Pigs that went through the hospital was 647 and, when they were all together, they were all young men, men with a tremendous sense of humour, and it was through this comradeship that they helped each other. It is remarkable that most of them have succeeded in life whereas really you would have expected them to fail. I think we can be of great value to other people in this respect."

Jim Sandiman Allen: "I thoroughly enjoyed just helping others and we all had to put a little bit back because, my God, when you look at it, a lot was done for us."

Derek Martin: "It gives one a feeling of comradeship, everyone is in much the same boat. We have all suffered the kind of experiences that other people could never experience perhaps. That gives us the sense of community and a sense of feeling. I suppose in me personally, it has given me a desire to want to help other people."

Percy Jayes: "Very exciting times, because one got tremendous experience within a very short space of time because of the volume of the work which, in peace time, would have been difficult to acquire, comparing to that sort of experience in that time."

Hank Hastings: "Happy experience in a difficult situation and ones that made you realise how fortunate you were to be alive and thankful that you had the expertise of people who really cared about you."

Jimmy Wright: "I think Archy McIndoe instilled that spirit of confidence that we were going to overcome the problems some how or another. If a chap had no hands and could not do up his button then we would help; we would help each other."

Tom Gleave: "Everyone is different. They all have funny ideas and funny ways and funny reactions, but we had a common thread you see. When you have been fried or mutilated, you develop something; you see another man and you immediately want to go and help him. The club is marvellous, but the entrance card comes at a high price."

Sister Meely: "There were so many happy times there. All the time, it was really funny."

Cyril Jones: "I could not think of anything that I would prefer to do. We did not make any money out of it, I shall not die a rich person, but I shall die a very satisfied person."

Ann Standen: "Who knows what battles go on when they have left, Archy, who knows?"

The Burns Unit still exists at the Queen Victoria Hospital. Sir Archibald McIndoe's portrait hangs in the reception as a proud reminder to all who pass through. As for Ward 3, the building still remains, although it is undergoing conversion work to a more practical use. In a few years, the Guinea Pig Club will cease to exist, but the brilliant and innovative surgery that was performed here in those early years will be remembered forever, and those brave young men who passed through will always be remembered for not going down to defeat, but for rising from defeat and bringing the spirit of victory back to the nation.

APPENDIX 1
THE ADVANCE OF PLASTIC SURGERY THROUGH THE AGES

The word plastic is derived from the Greek word 'plastikos', meaning to mould or give form. The true origins of plastic and reconstructive surgery go further back than most of us would think. Some historians trace the foundations as far back as the early Papyri of Egypt and the Sanskrit texts of ancient India. Within these early Hindu texts, which were possibly written more than 2,600 years ago, lie descriptions of nose, ear, and lip reconstructions using techniques ranging from pedicle flaps to free autogenous skin grafts.

The beginning of the Renaissance period in the 14th century brought a rebirth of science and medicine in general. Whilst the Middle Ages yielded only a few significant surgical developments, the reconstructive principles and techniques of the early Indian, Hellenistic, and Roman pioneers had been kept alive, passed on from generation to generation, and from one civilisation to another.

It was not until the end of the 18th century that reconstructive surgery began to resurface in Europe. As it formed, important changes were taking place that affected the entire nature of this unusual field. With the overall risks of surgery decreased through the use of anaesthesia and the development of the sterile technique by innovators such as Lister, the concept of performing surgery for reasons other than the reconstruction of damaged or altered parts of the body was at last permitted to exist in reality and in mind.

The modern specialty of plastic surgery that we know today owes much to a group of distinguished surgeons whose efforts in the first half of the twentieth century, notably during both World Wars, advanced and unified the subject. Vilray Papin Blair, an American surgeon from St Louis was one of these remarkable men, when in 1909 he published ground-breaking photographs of his efforts in reconstructive surgery. His contribution to the development of an effective military plastic surgical infrastructure during World War One was one of his greatest achievements. It allowed the military medical system to deal with the large volume of reconstructive cases produced by the effect of the war. When the United States entered the conflict in 1917, the Surgeon General established several sections under the division of surgery; including ophthalmology, otolaryngology, and head and neck surgery. For his accomplishments Blair was chosen to lead the section of head and neck surgery. Blair then persuaded the Surgeon General to change his title from Chief of Head and Neck Surgery to Chief of Plastic Surgery. This was a symbolic leap in terms of respectability in his chosen field.

During the Great War, the volume of injuries grew

considerably and in turn advanced most of the reconstructive surgery areas. A number of technical advances were achieved during this time. The work of reconstructive surgeons during World War One captured the attention and admiration of the public and academic world alike. Before the war, the use of crude facial masks to hide the disfigurements of wartime head and neck injuries was, essentially, the only option for those wishing to avoid the stares of society. These devices were made nearly obsolete through the efforts of plastic surgeons during the war. Lives were regained, hopes were restored and miracles were apparently occurring at the hands of surgeons. In essence, the war provided a backdrop by which surgeons could first begin to define the craft's realm and demonstrate its abilities to the world.

The defining moment for international plastic surgery did not arrive to its full extent until World War Two. Whist plastic surgery flourished in the United States between World War One and World War Two, its success was not as apparent in Europe and other parts of the world. Britain only had four dedicated plastic surgeons at the beginning of World War Two, these being McIndoe, Gillies, Kilner and Mowlem, compared with approximately sixty surgeons in the United States. However, World War Two produced a strong international growth of the field and by the end of the war the number of plastic surgeons in Britain had grown to twenty-five. In the United States, this number had reached one hundred and fifty.

Several medical advances enabled the extensive growth of the specialty during World War Two. Improvements in anaesthesia, more use of plasma for resuscitation, the use of sulphonamides and penicillin to control wound infections greatly contributed to the decrease in mortality and general look of plastic surgical procedures. In some military plastic surgery centres the mortality rate was down to zero.

The latter half of the 20th century saw tremendous growth in the specialty of plastic and reconstructive surgery. Currently, more than 5000 certified plastic surgeons perform more than 1.2 million procedures and more than 1 million cosmetic procedures each year in the United States alone. Both reconstructive and cosmetic surgeries have developed considerably over the past half-century and many new procedures and techniques are appearing.

APPENDIX 2
PROFILE OF SIR ARCHIBALD MCINDOE
(1900-1960)

Sir Archibald McIndoe was born on the 4th May 1900, the second of four children of John McIndoe, a printer from Dunedin, New Zealand. He attended Otago High School before studying medicine at Otago University. He qualified in 1924, winning medals in both medicine and surgery. After his studies he went on to be appointed house surgeon at Waikato Hospital. In the same year he was awarded the first New Zealand Fellowship at the Mayo Clinic in the United States, where he worked as a First Assistant in Pathological Anatomy for three years. During this period, he published several papers on hepatic disease including two individual papers on the importance of portal cirrhosis and on the structure of the bile canaliculus. He was subsequently awarded a John William White scholarship for foreign study and in 1929 was appointed first assistant in surgery at the Mayo Clinic. Whilst in America he met Lord Moynihan who was so impressed with his surgical skills that he recommended a permanent career in England.

McIndoe arrived in London in the winter of 1930. To his surprise there was no appointment available for him. On the suggestion of his cousin, Sir Harold

Gillies, he took up an appointment as clinical assistant in the Department of Plastic Surgery at St. Bartholomew's Hospital. He passed his FRCS examination in 1932 and shortly afterwards received his first permanent appointment as a General Surgeon and Lecturer at the Hospital for Tropical Diseases and the London School of Hygiene and Tropical Medicine. In 1934, he obtained the Fellowship of the American College of Surgeons. During his time in London he adapted himself to the technical demands of plastic surgery and in 1929 was appointed as a consultant plastic surgeon to St Bartholomew's Hospital, the Chelsea Hospital for Women, St. Andrew's Hospital, Hampstead Children's Hospital, the Royal North Stafford Infirmary and Croydon General Hospital.

McIndoe also held an appointment as a consultant in Plastic Surgery to the Royal Air Force and at the outbreak of World War II moved to the Queen Victoria Hospital at East Grinstead. This hospital had been rebuilt shortly before the outbreak of war and it possessed ample land for expansion to allow the establishment of a centre for plastic surgery. He strengthened his own position immensely by always resolutely refusing to be put into uniform. The work done by McIndoe in both physically and psychologically rehabilitating badly burned aircrew earned him an international reputation. McIndoe fought to improve the pay and conditions of badly injured airmen. 'The Guinea Pig Club' consisting of his ex-patients perpetuates his memory.

After the war many honours were bestowed upon him. He was appointed CBE in 1944, knighted in 1947 and received numerous foreign decorations. At the Royal College of Surgeons, he became a member of Council in 1946 and vice-president in 1958. He had been Hunterian Professor in 1939, and in 1958 was the Bradshaw Lecturer; his subject being facial burns. He helped to found the British Association of Plastic Surgeons and was its third President. McIndoe's brilliant career was no accident but due to a combination of factors. He was fortunate in being a cousin of Sir Harold Gillies, the doyen of plastic surgery, who persuaded him to forsake general for plastic surgery. McIndoe was a determined man who had the skill of getting what he wanted; even if it meant treading on other peoples toes. Forthright in expression, he was quick in making a decision. He had the great gift of an iron constitution coupled with an infinite capacity for hard work. McIndoe's contributions to plastic surgery are numerous. Most notably, he placed plastic surgery on a solid and permanent foundation. In July 1924 he married Adonia Aitken of Dunedin, by whom he had two daughters. The marriage was dissolved in 1953 and a year later in 1954, he remarried to Constance Belcham. He died in his sleep on 11th April 1960, his ashes being buried in the Royal Air Force church of St. Clement Danes, London. His memory lives on through all those that are treated and by the hard work carried out by the staff, at the Queen Victoria Hospital 'NHS Trust' based in East Grinstead, Southern England.

ACKNOWLEDGEMENTS

I would like to thank the Guinea Pig Club and all its friends and members who made this book possible.

With special thanks to the following:

The Queen Victoria Hospital, NHS Trust, East Grinstead
The Royal Air Force's Battle of Britain Association
Cyril Jones
Percy Jays
Sister Meely
Group Capt Thomas Gleave C.B.E.
Derek Martin
Jimmy White
Jack Allaway
Jim Sandiman Allen D.F.M.
Jack Toper
Hank Hastings
Bucky Alan Morgant
Julian Ankersmit
Annekin Wild
Sarah Merrill
Steve Connor
Alan Carr
Robert Garofalo
Lyn Beardsall
Jill Mullins
Ann Standen
Phin Hall

Artwork by Stuart Forrester

If you have enjoyed this book, please consider reviewing it on Amazon or Goodreads (or both)

And feel free visit the *Flying Machines And Their Heroes* website for other titles in this series and to receive a free audiobook:

flyingmachinesandtheirheroes.com

www.ingramcontent.com/pod-product-compliance
Lightning Source LLC
Chambersburg PA
CBHW071758040426
42446CB00012B/2612